This Book Belongs To:

....

....

....

First published in 2024

Copyright © Learn with Lolonyo

All rights reserved. No part of this book may be reproduced, scanned, stored in a retrieval system, or distributed in any form including printed or electronic without prior written permission from the author. Please do not participate in or encourage piracy of copyrighted materials.

Poems by Vivean Viola Pomell

Contents

I know Who I Am	4
I Love Writing Poetry	5
This Is Me	6
Summer Holiday Fun	7
Mommy & Daddy	8
Butterfly Wings	9
Dancing to the Rhythm	10
Simone & Cousin Beth	11
Goodbye Buggy	12
I Dream of Travelling	13
My School Days	14
Rising Above My Struggles	15
I Love Cricket	16

Grandpa & Grandma	17
I'm a Talented Painter	18
Facetime with Grandpa & Grandma	19
My Funny Story	20
The Environment Needs You	21
Keep Active	25
Genius in the Making	27
My Graduation Day	29
Musical Moments	30
I Am Destined to Succeed	32
Dreaming of a Pet	34
Time to Say Goodbye	36
Have a Go at Writing a Poem	38

I Know Who I Am

I am kind,
I am knowledgeable,
I am capable,
I know who I am.

I am beautiful,
I am blessed,
I am brave,
I know who I am.

I am clever,
I am courageous,
I am caring,
I know who I am.

I am loved,
I am always learning,
I am full of laughter,
I know just who I am.

I Love Writing Poetry

I love, I love writing poetry.
When I begin, there is no stopping me.

I like to think and use my imagination.
This is important when it comes to education.

I imagine I put all my words in a big pot,
Then get my wooden spoon and stir them a lot!

I mix over and over the rhythm and sounds,
Then something special is created, so I have found.

I hope you'll join me as I share my poems with you,
And perhaps, like me, you can get writing too.

This Is Me

My afro puffs are big, black, and puffy.
I love having my favourite style. "Thank you, Mommy."

Why do people ask if they can touch my hair?
I don't think so as this would be unfair.

I love the skin that I'm in,
A beautiful shade of brown,
That's my melanin!

I'm not as loud as you suppose,
I'm just energetic as I strike a pose.

I haven't got an attitude,
But I love to express my gratitude.

I appreciate all those who support me,
To be the very best that I can be.
This is me.

Summer Holiday Fun

I love to go to the beach for my summer holiday fun,
Making new friends each day as we play in the sun.
We get so excited as we feel the water between our toes,
Plant our buckets and spades and sand castles all in a row.
Splish and splash in the water as we cool ourselves down,
Then it's time for ice cream when we go into town.

Mommy & Daddy

M is for Mommy, so kind, loving, and protective.

D is for Daddy, who is strong, caring, and attentive.

Together, they help me in so many ways,

I look forward to this for many more days.

Butterfly Wings

If I had butterfly wings, I could do so many things.
Fly up into the clear blue sky until I am extremely high.

Summer gardens would be bright,
My beautiful wings would be a sight!

Now you can use your imagination,
And I'm sure you will agree,
You can be anything you dream you want to be.

Dancing to the Rhythm

Music makes me want to dance,
Music makes me skip and prance.
When I listen to the rhythm and rhyme,
My feet move to the beat every single time.
I can't help noticing it's my hands and legs too.
As Daddy plays the drums,
I hear a beat that's new.

Simone & Cousin Beth

This is Simone with her little cousin, Beth.
Biscuits and cakes are some of the things they like best.
When they finish baking, they always tidy up and pack away,
Ready for the next time, and then it's time to play.

Goodbye Buggy

I no longer need my buggy as I like to walk.
When going to the park, it's always good to talk.
Chatting about the many things we see on our way,
Like how many minibeasts we can spot in a single day.
I enjoy my favourite treat, chocolate ice cream.
Then, on our walk home, it's time to daydream.

I Dream of Travelling

I often dream of travelling by train
And then perhaps by aeroplane,
Discovering the various places that can be seen by bus
And exploring by tram the many cities around us.
These are just some of the journeys I could take
And keep all of the details in a journal I plan to make.

Go to school and do your best.

Enjoy learning, and we all will be impressed

With the efforts you make to listen and learn,

As you discover new things, share, and take turns!

Rising Above My Struggles

I will rise above my struggles

And appreciate all those cuddles.

Every time I overcome,

There is so much love that it weighs a ton.

I Love Cricket

Visits to my Uncle Henry are always so much fun.
I get to play my favourite game and eat some Jamaican bun.

When I visit on Saturdays, there's always time for a game of cricket.
Whenever I play, I try not to put my leg before the wicket.

My Grandad was the captain of the West Indies cricket team.
I'll never forget watching him win a match, which was my dream.

Grandpa & Grandma

Grandpa and Grandma's Sunday treat is jerk chicken and sorrel juice.
I can't wait for what comes next: my favourite dessert, chocolate mousse.

Grandpa always tells us stories of how he and Grandma met.
It was when Grandma was on her way with her cat to the vet.

Amazingly, they've been married for fifty years.
They had a big celebration, and my mom was so happy she shed a few tears.

When I sleep over, often just before it's time to sleep,
Grandma will tell me a story, especially one about a singing sheep.

Mommy says I can plan a special surprise for both of them.
I have a good idea, and on our next visit, I think we'll do it then.

I'm a Talented Painter

There are so many colours in my paint palette
Mom says I'm good at painting and that I've got talent.

I'm deciding which of my favourite things to paint
I guess that flying my kite will have to wait.

I mix the paints and try not to splash too far
And when I finally finish my beautiful flowers I say, "Ta-da"!

FaceTime with Grandpa & Grandma

I love my grandpa and grandma so much,
I'm always excited to keep in touch.
FaceTime is my favourite as I can see their faces,
Even though we are in different places.

My Funny Story

I wrote a funny story once, which I read aloud,
To my lovely teddy bears, mummy said I was allowed.

They liked my story so very much that I read it at show and tell,
Where the children laughed so much, and my teacher said I read well.

It's time to write another story to read to all my friends
Who are coming to my birthday party, I think I'll save it for the end.

I think I'll write about the big birthday surprise,
And when I've read it aloud, I'll say my goodbyes.

The Environment Needs You

There are many things that I can do
To care for the environment, but I need your help, too.

Recycle instead of binning household waste.
A recycled lunchbox does not alter the taste.

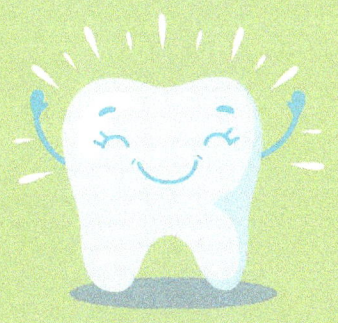

Brush your teeth, then turn off the tap
And unused switches before taking a nap.

Turn off the television if no one is viewing,
Including lights that no one is using.

For fertiliser, we make compost from unwanted peelings.
You can use this to grow fruits and vegetables,
Seeing them grow creates a wonderful feeling.

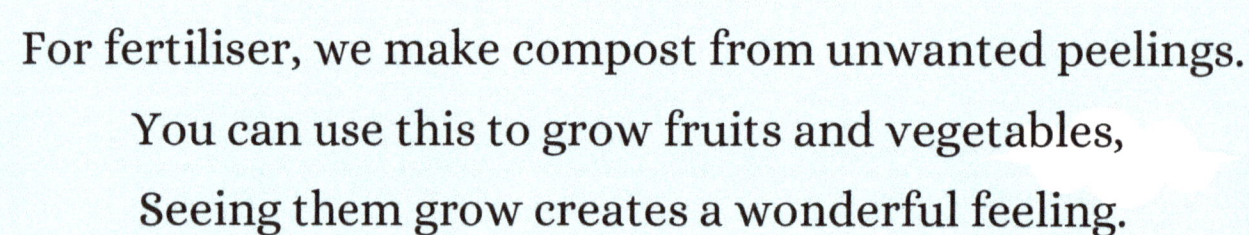

Going for a family walk is so much more fun
Than taking a ride in the car, where you cannot run.
We look forward to holding hands with Mom and Dad,
And watching the excitement of our pet dog, Zad.

Keep Active

Keeping active is what I try to do,
As my grandma says, "It's good for you."

I really enjoy going for a swim
On a sunny day to cool down my skin.

There is so much to see when you take a walk in the park,
Just make sure you're back before it's dark.

There are so many games and fun things to do,
Which ones you choose is really up to you.

Genius in the Making

I'm a genius in the making,

And that's because I'm always taking

Note of all the things I read

On my computer, in books, and in magazines.

School is where I do much learning.

It's most certainly not boring.

My teacher tells me I must use my brain

As there's lots of information to retain.

Sightseeing, libraries, and galleries

Are some of my favourite activities.

I learn so much about the world around us,

Valuing each other has got to be a bonus.

My Graduation Day

Aunty Clarice always calls me her little professor.
Dad often says I couldn't be anything lesser.
Perhaps, one day, I'll become just this,
I'll share all my knowledge. Won't this be sheer bliss?

Musical Moments

It's so much fun when I dance with my friends,
As we play so many instruments without end.
This gives me a very happy face,
And the sad feeling disappears without a trace.

Together, we dance to the musical beat,
Twisting our waist as we move our feet!
All cultures of the world make different music.
Some say these sounds can be very therapeutic!

I Am Destined to Succeed

I am confident, and I am also strong,

Some may say differently, but they are wrong.

My ability is not based on their opinion;

As my Mom tells me, I'm one in a million.

I've surprised both friends and family,

As I'm getting to where I'm destined to be.

Those around me will be able to tell,

As I continue, no doubt, to excel!

Dreaming of a pet

I sometimes ask Daddy if we can stop
When we are passing by the local pet shop,
As I often dream of having a pet,
And wonder which one of these I should get.
Perhaps it could be a goldfish or two,
Or a tortoise, hamster, or cockatoo.

A dog I can take on walks
Is much easier than riding a horse.

Spiders are too hairy for me,
But a cat can sit on my knee.

Dreams sometimes come true,
And they can too for me and you.

Time to Say Goodbye

Goodbye is something I don't like to say.
Somehow, I wish that we all could stay,
Learning more about words and sounds,
Imagination takes us to where rhythm can be found.

But take care until again we meet,
When I will have for you another treat.
Who knows, you may have a surprise for me too,
A number of poems written by you!

Have a go at Writing a Poem

Have a go at Writing a Poem

Have a go at Writing a Poem

Have a go at Writing a Poem

Have a go at Writing a Poem

Have a go at Writing a Poem

Have a go at Writing a Poem

Have a go at Writing a Poem

Have a go at Writing a Poem

Have a go at Writing a Poem

Have a go at Writing a Poem

Have a go at Writing a Poem

Have a go at Writing a Poem

Have a go at Writing a Poem

Have a go at Writing a Poem

Have a go at Writing a Poem

Have a go at Writing a Poem

Have a go at Writing a Poem

Have a go at Writing a Poem

Have a go at Writing a Poem

Have a go at Writing a Poem

Have a go at Writing a Poem

Have a go at Writing a Poem

Have a go at Writing a Poem

Have a go at Writing a Poem

Have a go at Writing a Poem

Have a go at Writing a Poem

Have a go at Writing a Poem

Have a go at Writing a Poem

Have a go at Writing a Poem

Have a go at Writing a Poem

Have a go at Writing a Poem

Have a go at Writing a Poem

Have a go at Writing a Poem

www.ingramcontent.com/pod-product-compliance
Lightning Source LLC
Chambersburg PA
CBHW042354070526
44585CB00028B/2923